IT'S NOT ALL RIGHT TO BE A FOSTER KID....

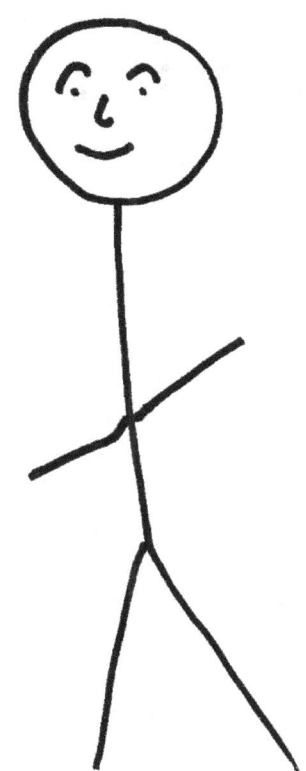

.....no matter what they say

"Every time we turn our heads the other way when we see the law flouted, when we tolerate what we know to be wrong, when we close our eyes and ears to the corrupt because we are too busy or too frightened, when we fail to speak up and speak out, we strike a blow against freedom and decency and justice." **Robert F. Kennedy**

INTRODUCTION

I spent my childhood, from age seven through seventeen, in foster care. Over the course of those ten years, many decent, well-meaning, and concerned people told me, "It's okay to be foster kid."

In saying that, those very good people meant to encourage me, and I appreciated their kindness then, and all these many decades later, I still appreciate their good intentions. But as I was tossed around the foster care system, it began to dawn on me that they were wrong. It was not all right to be a foster kid.

During my time in the system, I was bounced every eighteen months from three foster homes to an orphanage to a boy's school and to a group home before I left on my own accord at age seventeen.

In the course of my stay in foster care, I was severely beaten in two homes by my "care givers" and separated from my four siblings who were also in care, sometimes only blocks away from where I was living.

I left the system rather than to wait to age out, although the effects of leaving the system without any family, means, or safety net of any kind, were the same as if I had aged out. I lived in poverty for the first part of my life, dropped out of high school, and had continuous problems with the law.

I left foster care in 1972. Yet, today, almost nothing about foster care has changed. Exactly what happened to me is happening to some other child, somewhere in America, right now. The system, corrupt, bloated, and inefficient, goes on, unchanging and secretive.

Something has gone wrong in a system that was originally a compassionate social policy built to improve lives but is now a definitive cause in ruining lives. Due to gross negligence, mismanagement, apathy, and greed, mostly what the foster care system builds are dangerous consequences. Truly, foster care has become our epic national disgrace and a nightmare for those of us who have lived through it.

Yet there is a suspicion among some Americans that foster care costs too much, undermines the work ethic, and is at odds with a satisfying life. Others see foster care as a part of the welfare system, as legal plunder of the public treasuries.

None of that is true; in fact, all that sort of thinking does is to blame the victims. There is not a single child in the system who wants to be there or asked to be there. Foster kids are in foster care because they had nowhere else to go. It's that simple. And believe me, if those kids could get out of the system and be reunited with their parents and lead normal, healthy lives, they would. And if foster care is a sort of legal plunder of the public treasuries, it's not the kids in the system who are doing the plundering.

We need to end this needless suffering. We need to end it because it is morally and ethically wrong and because the generations to come will not judge us on the might of our armed forces or our technological advancements or on our fabulous wealth.

Rather, they will judge us, I am certain, on our compassion for those who are friendless, on our decency to those who have nothing and on our efforts, successful or not, to make our nation and our world a better place. And if we cannot accomplish those things in the short time allotted to us, then let them say of us "at least they tried."

You can change the tragedy of foster care and here's how to do it. We have created this book so that almost all of it can be tweeted out by you to the world. You have the power to improve the lives of those in our society who are least able to defend themselves. All you need is the will to do it.

If the American people, as good, decent and generous as they are, knew what was going on in foster care, in their name and with their money, they would stop it. But, generally speaking, although the public has a vague notion that foster care is a mess, they don't have the complete picture. They are not aware of the human, economic and social cost that the mismanagement of the foster care system puts on our nation.

By tweeting the facts laid out in this work, you can help to change all of that. You can make a difference. You can change things for the better.

We can always change the future for a foster kid; to make it better ...you have the power to do that. Speak up (or tweet out) because it's your country. Don't depend on the "The other guy" to speak up for these kids, because you are the other guy.

We cannot build a future for foster children, but we can build foster children for the future and the time to start that change is today.

Different studies all say the same thing, that it's not all right to be a foster kid (Tweet it!)

A study of the long-term homeless in Minneapolis found that 39 % had experienced foster care or institutional care as children. (Tweet it!)

ACLU estimates that a child in state care is 10 times more likely to be abused than one in the care of his parents. (Tweet it!)

ACLU on foster kids. In the name of protecting children, we have kept it a secret how we as a society deal with our most vulnerable children (Tweet it!)

ACLU on foster kids. There is a great gap between protecting a child's identity and keeping the acts of our government secret (Tweet it!)

ACLU on foster kids. Any time you take a system and cloak it in secrecy there are going to be substantial abuses (Tweet it!)

ACLU on foster kids. Department of Social Services is often too quick to take custody of children away from their parents. (Tweet it!)

ACLU on foster kids Foster care systems are cloaked in secrecy that often is used to conceal illegal and unconscionable practices. (Tweet it!)

Association for Children: 75% of the 772 respondents rated Massachusetts, the Department of Social Services as inadequate (Tweet it!)

Child Welfare League of America: Typical foster parent is a single, low income, low educated woman, already mother of 2 (Tweet it!)

COLA: Many foster parents illiterate with poorly developed reading skills. (Tweet it!)

Federal study of former foster kids found that one-fourth had been homeless, 40% were on public assistance, and half were unemployed. (Tweet it!)

Institute for Children and Poverty: Homeless families whose heads of households grew up in foster care are at greatest risk of dissolution. (Tweet it!)

MIT: kids placed in foster care by caseworkers more likely to have run-ins with the law less likely employed than kids left with families. (Tweet it!)

MIT: Foster children about 3 times more likely to become delinquents/ adult criminals than children who are kept with their families. (Tweet it!)

MIT: Girls placed in foster care are nearly twice as likely to become teenage mothers (Tweet it!)

MIT: children placed in foster homes are also less likely to be employed and earn less than those who are kept in their homes. (Tweet it!)

MIT: state agencies should devote more resources to treating and meeting the needs of families rather than resorting to foster care. (Tweet it!)

National Association of Social Workers, 20 % of children living in runaway shelters come directly from foster care. (Tweet it!)

A survey also found that 80% of prisoners in **Illinois** spent time in foster care as children. (Tweet it!)

A lawsuit in **Fla**. found that 73% of the states children graduate high school less than half the states foster children would graduate. (Tweet it!)

New York City Study found that 27% of the aged out males and 10% of the females had been incarcerated (Tweet it)

New York City Study found that 33% of the aged out were receiving public assistance (Tweet it!)

New York City Study found that 37% of the aged out had not finished high school (Tweet it!)

New York City Study found that 50% of the aged out were unemployed (Tweet it!)

New York City a study determined that between 25 – 50% of the young men in the homeless shelters were former foster care wards. (Tweet it!)

Survey by NASW: 20% of children living in runaway shelters come directly from foster care. (Tweet it!)

Survey by NASW: 80% of prisoners in Illinois and California spent time in foster care as children. (Tweet it!)

Study in the **Minneapolis** area found that between 14 and 26% of homeless adults were former foster care children. (Tweet it!)

Study in Calgary found that 90% of street kids had been in foster care prior to winding up living on the streets. (Tweet it!)

U.S. Ways and Means: majority foster children come from families supported by Aid to Families with Dependent Children (Tweet it!)

U.S. Ways and Means 46% of the foster care population are minority children. (Tweet it!)

Yale University: "children who spend years drifting between foster care homes can't be expected to be healthy. (Tweet it!)

Westat: 54% of Foster kids had completed high school, 49% were employed 38% maintained a job for at least 1 year 40% cost the community (Tweet it!)

The bottom line............. "I saw the injustice of it all, I thought 'Why doesn't somebody do something to stop that' but nobody did. Then I realized I was somebody' (Tweet it!)

HOW THE SYSTEM DOESN'T WORK

Child welfare systems often fail to initiate or complete investigations of abuse or neglect quickly enough — or to investigate at all. (Tweet it!)

Child welfare systems often fail to accurately assess children's risk of being harmed. (Tweet it!)

Child welfare systems often use poor decision-making about whether or not to remove children from their homes. (Tweet it!)

Child welfare systems often fail to adequately monitor families who are known to the child welfare system (Tweet it!)

Child welfare systems often fail to adequately train and supervise the social workers who respond to reports of maltreatment (Tweet it!)

Child welfare systems often fail to provide appropriate supervision after an investigation, putting kids in danger of further abuse. (Tweet it!)

Child welfare systems often fail to properly monitor foster homes and other placements. (Tweet it!)

Despite more than a decade of intended reform, the nation's foster care system is still overcrowded and rife with problems. (Tweet it!)

Many child welfare systems are underfunded, understaffed, serious system wide problems, lacking the leadership necessary to fix them. (Tweet it!)

There are no provisions for treatment, prevention, family support, or aging out -- just for supporting things as they are. (Tweet it!)

THE KIDS IN THE SYSTEM

THERE IS NO PICTURE HERE
BECAUSE IT DOESN'T MATTER WHAT KIND OF
KID THEY ARE.....THIER KIDS AND THEY
ARE IN PAIN AND WE NEED TO FIX THAT
BECAUSE WE ARE ALL CHILDREN God

General make up of foster kids year after year is 40% White, 30% Black, 20% Hispanic, 10% all others (Tweet it!)

Numbers have consistently shown a slightly greater percentage of boys than girls in foster care. (Tweet it!)

Average Age of foster kids: 10.0 years
6% 1 year
26% 1-5 years
20% 6-10 years
28% 11-15 years
18% 16-18 years
2% 19 years
(Tweet it!)

Gender of foster children
Male 52%
Female 48%
(Tweet it!)

Of the estimated 423,773 children in foster care on September 30, 2009, 53% were male and 47% were female. (Tweet it!)

Foster kid: A file number, another kid in the system, bound to fail, not a human being with a potentially bright future. (Tweet it!)

At any given time in America, there are about 500,000 children in foster care. About half of that number will have a temporary stay (Tweet it!)

About 150,000 kids will remain in the system for six years or longer, some for their entire childhoods. (Tweet it!)

Foster care is, as one child put it "punishment for something you didn't do" (Tweet it!)

Something has gone wrong in what was originally a compassionate social policy meant to improve the lives of others. (Tweet it!)

Largely what the foster care system has done is to breed dangerous and perverse consequences. (Tweet it!)

A large part of the problem is that the system is self - perpetuating. (Tweet it!)

Foster care is an unnatural state (Tweet it!)

The chief aim of the foster care system isn't to foster or care but to reduce children to a level of complete dependence (Tweet it!)

The system is overloaded because it is badly managed (Tweet it!)

The cookie cutter mentality is hard at work in foster care. (Tweet it!)

Foster placement is not individualized for the child's best interest, seldom maximizes the healing aspects these kids need (Tweet it!)

40% of foster children are white; 34% are black; 18% are Hispanic. (Tweet it!)

The average age of a foster child is 10. Half are 10 or under. (Tweet it!)

On any given day, there are approximately 424,000 children in out-of-home care in the United States. (Tweet it!)

During the last year (almost any year) about 680,000 children spent some time in out-of-home care in the United States. (Tweet it!)

1,200 children enter foster care each day remaining there on average for more than two years. (Tweet it!)

The number of children in foster care has declined nationally each year since 2005. (Tweet it!)

More than half of all foster kids live in nine states: California Florida Illinois Indiana Michigan New York Ohio, Pennsylvania, and Texas. (Tweet it!)

The average age of the children in foster care is just over nine years old. (Tweet it!)

The median amount of time children spent in foster care increased between 2000 (12 months) and 2010 (15.4 months). (Tweet it!)

On average, children in the American child welfare systems spend more than two years — 26.7 months — in foster care. (Tweet it!)

11% of children in foster care have languished there for five or more years. (Tweet it!)

While most children in foster care live in family settings, a substantial minority 16% live in institutions and group homes. (Tweet it!)

About 70,000 children living in foster care have had their biological parents rights permanently terminated. (Tweet it!)

Most children are placed in foster care temporarily due to parental abuse or neglect. (Tweet it!)

A record 304,000 children entered the system in 2004, according to one study. Much of the rise was due to methamphetamine use. (Tweet it!)

Experts estimate that 80 to 90% of foster care placements can be traced to substance abuse. (Tweet it!)

About 40,000 infants are placed in foster care every year. (Tweet it!)

IT'S ESPECIALLY NOT GOOD TO BE A BLACK CHILD IN THE FOSTER CARE SYSTEM

Black children are more likely than other children to be reported, investigated, substantiated, and placed in foster care. (Tweet it!)

Black children stay longer in care and are less likely to be reunified with their families. (Tweet it!)

31% of the children in foster care are African American, double the percent of African American children in the population in America. (Tweet it!)

While African American children are overrepresented in child welfare system in every state, Asian children tend to be underrepresented. (Tweet it!)

Children of color, especially black children, and American Indian children, face significant disparity within the child welfare system. (Tweet it!)

At the turn of the century more than half of the children entering foster care in the U.S. were children of color. (Tweet it!)

Children of color are more likely to have longer placements in foster care than white children (Tweet it!)

Children of color are less likely to receive comprehensive services in foster care than white children (Tweet it!)

Children of color are less likely to reunify with their families than white children. (Tweet it!)

The rates of child welfare involvement for black and American Indian children are more than twice those of white children. (Tweet it!)

California study, 2 in 5 black children were likely to experience child welfare involvement by age 7 (Tweet it!)

California study 1 in 10 black children was likely to experience at least one foster care placement. (Tweet it!)

There is a strong correlation between race and permanent placement. (Tweet it!)

Black children are adopted at the same rate as other races, but the process takes longer, with less chance of reunification with parents. (Tweet it!)

Black and/or Hispanic children are less likely to be reunified with their families than other children in the foster care system. (Tweet it!)

ABUSE

Children are 11 times more likely to be abused in State care than they are in their own homes. (Tweet it!)

Children died because of abuse in foster care 5.25 times more often than children in the general population. (Tweet it!)

Foster care is intended to protect children yet too often, it becomes an equally cruel form of neglect and abuse by the state (Tweet it!)

The number of abuse/ neglect related incidents that occur in foster care is difficult to determine.

Confidentiality laws shield agencies from public scrutiny. (Tweet it!)

There is no shortage of abuse cases in foster care that make it to the light of day. (Tweet it!)

Children removed from abusive homes are being abused by a system designed to protect them. (Tweet it!)

Many of America's foster children have been victims of repeated abuse and prolonged neglect. The system does the same thing. (Tweet it!)

Many child welfare systems overmedicate children to control their behavior. (Tweet it!)

Many child welfare systems fail to protect children in foster care from further abuse and neglect. (Tweet it!)

Many child welfare systems compound the trauma that abused and neglected children have already experienced (Tweet it!)

AGED OUT

(Aged out" means that when foster kids reach age 18 and they are emancipated from foster care and left on their own with no support...Tweet it)

Each year about 20,000 kids age out 70% will have no place to live no prospects, no skills to deal with even mildly problematic situations (Tweet it!)

Generally, foster children don't know how to anticipate for the future, it's beyond them. (Tweet it!)

More than 20,000 children each year never leave the system -- they remain in foster care until they "age out." (Tweet it!)

Of the 460,000 children in foster care currently, 26,000 have a case goal of emancipation.(This figure won't change much over the decades) (Tweet it!)

Studied aged out foster kids were twice as likely as same-age peers in the national sample to have a child. (Tweet it!)

Aging out of foster care without a permanent family means having no one to share your life with (Tweet it!)

Aging out of foster care has harmful long-term effects on kids (Tweet it!)

Maine and Virginia, more than 20% who exited foster care in 2004 because they aged out. (Tweet it!)

Children often find themselves with no connection to reliable adults and few supports when they are forced to exit foster care. (Tweet it!)

"If I don't have my car payment this month, that's it; it's not like I can ask anyone for money. We don't have much to fall back on." (Tweet it!)

Aged out kids feel scared, uncertain, alone, unprepared to handle everyday life. (Tweet it!)

"I didn't meet with anybody about what was going to happen when I aged out" (Tweet it!)

"I didn't know what programs would be available to me, I didn't know what I was going to have to do" (Tweet it!)

Aged out Foster kid "You're trying to get through the day, and you don't even have time to think about the future". (Tweet it!)

Aged out Foster kid: "You're so worried about 'Am I going to have a place to live?' Am I going to get kicked out?" (Tweet it!)

The percentage of youth that age out of foster care has increased. (Tweet it!)

Various studies of young people who have aged out of foster care without a permanent family: 12-30% struggled with homelessness. (Tweet it!)

30% of the homeless in America and some 25 % of those in prison were once in foster care. (Tweet it!)

Various studies of young people who have aged out of foster care without a permanent family: 40-63% did not complete high school (Tweet it!)

Aged out kids without a permanent family: 25-55 % were unemployed (Tweet it!)

Aged out kids employed had average earnings below the poverty level (Tweet it!)

Only 38% of aged out kids were still working after one year out of care (Tweet it!)

Various studies of aged out foster kids: 30-62% had trouble accessing health care due to finances/lack of insurance (Tweet it!)

Various studies of aged out foster kids 40% were forced to rely on public assistance and 50% experienced extreme financial hardship (Tweet it!)

Various studies of aged out of foster kids without a permanent family: 31-42% had been arrested after foster care ended (Tweet it!)

Various studies of aged out of foster kids care without a permanent family: 18-26% were incarcerated(Tweet it!)

Various studies of aged out foster kids 40-60% of the young women were pregnant within 12-18 months of leaving foster care. (Tweet it!)

CIRCLE GAME

It is a circle game. Former foster kids twice as likely as parents with no such history to see their own children placed in foster care (Tweet it!)

Damaged foster kids will be damaged adults who will continue to lead tragic lives and will increasingly tax our public resources. (Tweet it!)

People who grew up in foster care twice more likely to lose at least one child to foster care. (Tweet it!)

Young adults leaving foster-care are ill equipped for life on their own & often end up homeless or permanently dependent on welfare (Tweet it!)

It is a circle game and it is hidden from the public. These dreadful statistics of foster care have not changed in decades (Tweet it!)

CRIME

Foster youth who age out often grim ends: 1 in 4 will be jailed within the first 2 years after they leave the system. (Tweet it!)

Connecticut officials estimate 75% of youths in the state's criminal justice system were once in foster care. (Tweet it!)

California study found that a third of children placed in foster care eventually end up homeless, and 35% are arrested while in foster care (Tweet it!)

28% of studied aged out kids reported having been arrested and almost 20% had been incarcerated (Tweet it!)

DRUGS/ ALCOHOL ADDICTION

Children placed in out-of-home care, regardless of the reason, are at higher risk of developing alcohol/ drug problems (Tweet it!)

People who grew up in foster care are 30% more likely to be substance abusers (Tweet it!)

DEATH

2.1% of all child fatalities took place in foster care. The contrast in population general pop 99.6%, only 4% in state care (Tweet it!)

Children die in foster care and they always have. (Tweet it!)

In Massachusetts, in one year, at least eight children died while in foster care. (Tweet it!)

Two year period in Arizona one foster child died every seven weeks, four were "viciously beaten to death" by foster parents. (Tweet it!)

Nationwide in a two-year period, one foster child died on average every seven and a half weeks. (Tweet it!)

District Judge: If you take on the responsibility to take care of someone (in foster care) the least we can ask is that they come out of it alive. (Tweet it!)

EDUCATION OR LACK THEREOF

A large portion of the half million children in foster care perform poorly in school and more likely to have behavior/ discipline problems (Tweet it!)

This year (it doesn't matter which year you are reading this) foster children are more likely than other kids to drop out of school (Tweet it!)

Various studies indicate children in foster care tend to perform poorly in school compared to children who are not in foster care (Tweet it!)

Studies indicate that children in foster care tend to lag behind in their education by at least one year (Tweet it!)

Studies indicate that children and young people in foster care tend to have lower educational attainment than the general population. (Tweet it!)

13% of aged out foster children attend college 2% will actually graduate. They lack the basic educational skills and family support (Tweet it!)

Less than 1.5% of long term-aged out foster kids will attend graduate school. (Tweet it!)

73% of Fla. children graduate from high school, as opposed to less than half of foster children (Tweet it!)

Less than 54% of people who grew up in foster care will complete high school (Tweet it!)

Approximately 58% have a high school degree at age 19, compared to 87% of a national comparison group of non-foster youth. (Tweet it!)

Less than 3% earned their college degrees, compared with 28% of the general population. (Tweet it!)

Over 33% of studied aged out foster kids had not received a high school diploma or GED, compared to 10 % in the national sample. (Tweet it!)

Aged out foster kids completing a bachelor's or higher is approximately 2%, compared with a national rate of 24%.(Tweet it!)

Once they leave the system and they are never provided with a specialized educational or vocational training they'll need to survive after they become 18. (Tweet it!)

EFFECTS OF FOSTER CARE ON CHILDREN

This year (it doesn't matter which year you are reading this) former foster children will commit crimes, abuse drugs and become teen parents. (Tweet it!)

By the second or third year in foster care, many children mistake consequence for the failures of others as their fate. (Tweet it!)

Foster children often don't see things as they are; they see things as they are by the conditions that have set their perceptions (Tweet it!)

Many long-term foster children operate from a false sense of self, they believe it protects them from further hurt, rejection, and disappointment. (Tweet it!)

Foster children may feel embarrassed when confronted with questions from outsiders about their families (Tweet it!)

Many foster children are left to grow up without the abilities necessary to become successful in the adult world. (Tweet it!)

For many foster children, faith in the present dies quickly and faith in the future expires soon afterwards (Tweet it!)

A child with no psychological parents, adrift in the world is headed toward bad outcomes and society is going to pay for it. (Tweet it!)

The wounded foster child responds to the pain and anxiety in a different way (Tweet it!)

The wounded foster child holds the same wish for love, acceptance, carries the same fears of rejection, abandonment. (Tweet it!)

By definition, every foster child is an abandoned child who has suffered a devastating loss. (Tweet it!)

Study after study, even when foster kids are compared with other disadvantaged youth, the foster kid comes out worse. (Tweet it!)

Foster kids suffer a loss of the self, and a sense of incompleteness (Tweet it!)

Foster kids suffer a lack of wholeness, a sense that something is missing. (Tweet it!)

Foster kids are reluctant to trust others to be there for them. (Tweet it!)

Foster children have limited life experience to build on and to establish their sense of self. (Tweet it!)

The foster child responds to anxiety in different ways. Every child wishes for acceptance, each carries the fear of rejection (Tweet it!)

HOMELESSNESS

Individuals who grew up in foster care are 50% more likely to have a history of domestic violence than the overall homeless population. (Tweet it!)

Three of 10 of the nation's homeless are former foster children. (Tweet it!)

Up to 50% of former foster youth become homeless within the first 18 months of emancipation (Tweet it!)

11% of the youths in shelters said they were homeless and living on the streets before coming to shelters. (Tweet it!)

Some experts estimate that 45% of those leaving foster care become homeless within a year. (Tweet it!)

The disproportionate representation of former foster care children among the homeless population has long been documented. (Tweet it!)

A federal study of former foster care wards; one-fourth had been homeless (Tweet it!)

Some estimate that 45% of those leaving foster care become homeless within a year because they have no support system (Tweet it!)

Foster children are guaranteed to become America's homeless class. (Tweet it!)

Over one-fifth will become homeless at some time after age 18. (Tweet it!)

One in seven aged out kids reported experiencing homelessness at least once since discharge. (Tweet it!)

People who grew up in foster care 50% more likely to have a history of domestic violence than the overall homeless population. (Tweet it!)

More than one-third of runaway youth have been in foster care in the year before they took to the streets. (Tweet it!)

More than one out of five youths who arrive at a shelter come directly from a foster or group home (Tweet it!)

38% of runaways say they had been in foster care at some time during the previous year. (Tweet it!)

In Calgary an astounding 90% of street children had been in foster care prior to living on the streets (Tweet it!)

According to a nationwide study of runaway youths, more than one-third had been in foster care in the year before they took to the streets. (Tweet it!)

More than one out of five youths who arrive at a shelter comes directly from a foster or group home (Tweet it!)

38% in shelters nationwide say they had been in foster care at some time during the previous year (Tweet it!)

Here's the bottom line: Foster care has created a new class of American; the throwaway citizen whom everyone knows will probably go to a life of drugs, alcohol abuse, homelessness and crime (Tweet it!)

LEGAL KIDNAPPING

It's not exactly kidnapping....its...yeah, never mind, it's kidnapping.

"When you are taken to the system, at least allow us to go home and get some clothes." (Tweet it!)

"They came and got us from school. When they come to pick you up and take you it's like a raid." (Tweet it!)

In most states, allegations of abuse or neglect are not necessary to remove a child, or to permanently sever parental rights. (Tweet it!)

In virtually every state, laws allow the removal of children on the basis that they may be abused or neglected in the future. (Tweet it)

About half of the 500,000 children in foster care don't belong there. Half were in no immediate danger and could have been safely left in the care of their parents. (Tweet it!)

The risk of losing children to the state is something of an occupational hazard for poor mothers (Tweet it!)

The finding of neglect on a mother's part is just another word for impoverished. (Tweet it!)

Among the other problems a poor family faces, the state could take your kid. (Tweet it!)

A majority of foster children have been removed from their homes on the basis of questionable neglect charges (Tweet it!)

No matter what the caseworkers call it, relinquishment or surrender of parenthood, the child experiences it as abandonment. (Tweet it!)

LOST IN THE SYSTEM

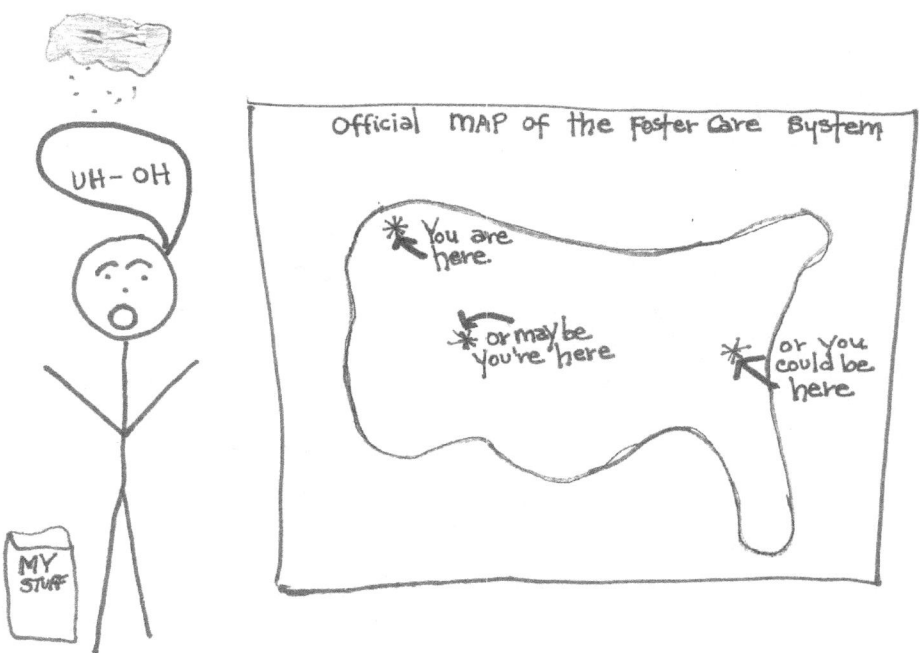

Children become lost in the foster care system and sometimes children die in the system. (Tweet it!)

LOW CALIBER
FOSTER HOMES

"Foster care is like Russian Roulette, any given foster home could well be 100% worse than the last home "(Tweet it!)

Some foster parents are in it for the money because once they receive their monthly payments there is no accounting for how the funds are used (Tweet it!)

It cannot be denied that financial gain is among a number of significant incentives leading some to become foster parents. (Tweet it!)

Children are put in inappropriate placements, not designed to offer family counseling, psychiatric treatment or drug treatment. **Dennis Lepak** (Tweet it!)

The quality of foster care homes has unquestionably diminished over the years. (Tweet it!)

Judge: The typical foster parent I see is a single woman who has several biological children, supported by welfare or disability. (Tweet it!)

Judge: The typical foster parent I see is a high school dropout whose own kids are marginally functioning. (Tweet it!)

Judge: The typical foster parent I sees does not have the ability to help (The kids) with their schoolwork (Tweet it!)

Judge: The typical foster parent I see has little hope for a brighter economic or social future. (Tweet it!)

Recruit foster parents from the public assistance rolls (Tweet it!)

Massachusetts: 41% of foster homes run by single parents, many of whom care for several foster children in addition to their own. (Tweet it!)

Once foster families receive their monthly payments, no accounting for how the funds are used is actually required in most cases. (Tweet it!)

Mental Illness

The system is overwhelmed and ill prepared to provide mental health needs for foster kids (Tweet it!)

States are more successful in finding permanent homes for the general foster care population than for children with a diagnosed disability (Tweet it!)

About half of children under five years old in foster care have developmental delays. (Tweet it!)

Up to 80% of all children in foster care have serious emotional problems. (Tweet it!)

One finding was that a number of adolescents in foster care were suffering from severe, but treatable, psychiatric disorders which had gone undetected. (Tweet it!)

The definition of youth is life as yet untouched by tragedy which is why most foster children can't ever remember being young. (Tweet it)

More than half of studied aged out foster kids reported clinical levels of at least one mental health issue in the last month, with 20% reporting three or more mental health issues. (Tweet it!)

Foster children usually suffer from psychiatric illness-depression, anxiety, ADD (Tweet it!)

Foster kids suffer, even when the cause of suffering is over they suffer, long after they have forgotten what they are suffering about. (Tweet it!)

What we recall from our childhoods we recall forever, for foster kids those memories are nightmares. (Tweet it!)

Foster children carry with them the worst guilt of all, unearned guilt. (Tweet it!)

Mental disturbances were found in 57% of a study group of foster children in foster homes but leaped to 96% in group home children (Tweet it!)

Many of America's foster children have not experienced a nurturing, stable environment and usually have unmet mental health needs. (Tweet it!)

Foster care kids are three to six times more likely than children not in care to have emotional, behavioral, and developmental problems (Tweet it!)

Foster care kids 6 Xs more likely to have conduct disorders, depression, difficulties in school impaired social relationships. (Tweet it!)

Multiple placements, each school transfer brings a new set of adjustments that impede academic progress and social relations. (Tweet it!)

Estimates are that about 30% of foster children have marked or severe emotional problems. (Tweet it!)

33% of studied aged out foster kids reported mental health issues, including PTSD, major depression, and alcohol and substance abuse. (Tweet it!)

25% of studied aged out foster kids experiencing PTSD symptoms. (Tweet it!)

Focus group in California noted that negative effects from being in foster care will stay with them for the rest of their lives. (Tweet it!)

If you came out of foster care with dependencies and issues, unresolved issues that you will carry around into your adulthood (Tweet it!)

It depends on the individual, but a lot of foster kids, have the same baggage. (Tweet it!)

Many foster children grow up to become adults who vent their rage and frustration on society with violence. (Tweet it!)

The bottom Line............ Kids cannot change the problems with being in foster care until they accept it, that acceptance, a foster kid's reality, can be terrifying. (Tweet it!)

Poor health

Nearly half of all children in foster care have chronic medical problems. (Tweet it!)

US GAO examined whether US foster children were being adequately serviced in health care needs and found 12% receive no routine care. (Tweet it!)

US GAO found that 34% of foster kids receive no immunizations 32% have some identified health needs that are not met. (Tweet it!)

US GAO found that 78% of foster kids are at high risk for human immunodeficiency virus because of parental drug abuse, yet only 9% are tested for HIV. (Tweet it!)

Many child welfare systems fail to provide adequate medical, dental, and mental health services to ensure children's health & well-being (Tweet it!)

Misdirected Guidelines and Treatments

Federal guidelines encourage foster care programs to emphasize short-term, crisis-management services which does little for foster children (Tweet it!)

Misdirected Finances

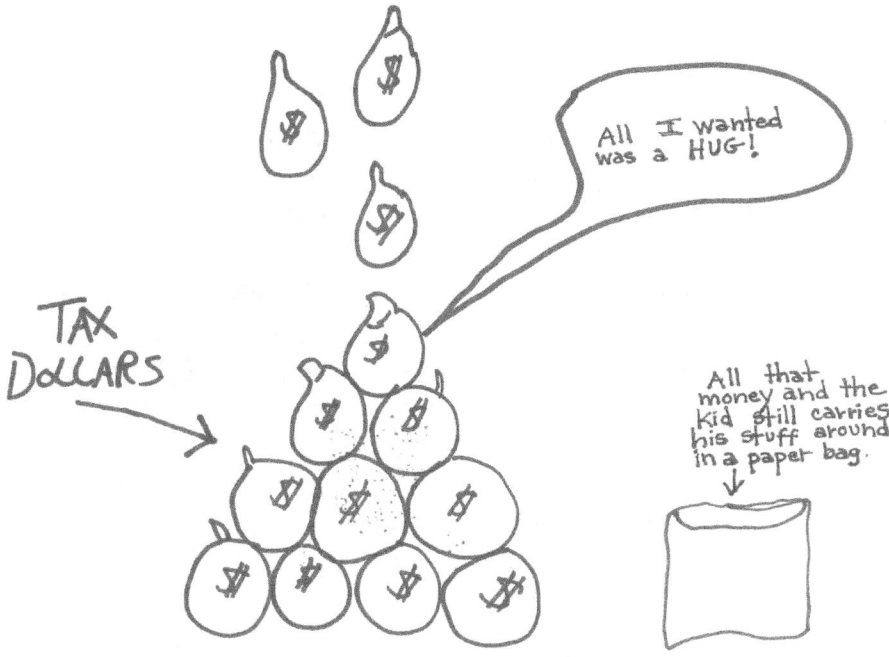

Taxpayers are spending $22 billion a year -- or $40,000 a child -- on foster care programs that probably don't work (Tweet it!)

The problem is the continued flow of federal cash into the system, although well intended, only contributes to the foster care crisis. (Tweet it!)

About half of the children now in foster care could be in their own homes if proper services were underwritten (Tweet it!)

We now spend eight times more on children in foster care than on services to keep children out of foster care. (Tweet it!)

Funds allocated to in-home services are being diverted instead to foster care. About half the children in care could be in their own homes (Tweet it!)

Foster care systems established and funded to serve children are failing, producing more damaged kids who will produce new generations of damaged kids (Tweet it!)

The people we hire to spend the foster funds spend the money where it would best service them and not US...me you and foster kids (Tweet it!)

Funds already allocated by the federal government to in-home services are being diverted instead to foster care. (Tweet it!)

Permanency

Many child welfare systems are warehousing children in institutions, group homes, emergency shelters, and other "temporary" non-family settings. (Tweet it!)

Children abused or neglected have a heightened need for permanency, security, emotional constancy. The state answers that by moving the child around. (Tweet it!)

"Foster care drift" that about says it all. (Tweet it!)

Child welfare bounce children from unstable placements uprooting their lives without warning, reducing the chance for a permanent home. (Tweet it!)

Children have on average three different foster care placements. (Tweet it!)

Frequent moves in and out of the homes of strangers can be profoundly unsettling for children (Tweet it!)

The only consistent thing about being a foster child is knowing that you're going to be moved. (Tweet it!)

Repeated moves add to the problem of foster kids general inability to cope with life situation lessons. (Tweet it!)

Foster kids are human basketballs, getting tossed around from one place to another (Tweet it!)

A permanent and loving family is important to grow and thrive, but the need for a family doesn't end when a child turns 18. (Tweet it!)

Foster children's sense of time focuses exclusively on the present and has only a minimal understanding of temporary versus permanent. (Tweet it!)

Youth who age out of foster care without the support of a permanent family are quickly confronted with the realities of life on their own. (Tweet it!)

Instability is seen in extraordinarily high incidence of drug abuse, homelessness, psych problems among former foster children. (Tweet it!)

The system generally fails to move kids quickly into permanent homes through reunification or adoption (Tweet it!)

The bottom line.............A foster kid is just a kid, they deserve what every other child has: a permanent, safe, loving family on whom they can count on in their adult years. (Tweet it!)

Poor placement

The child's attachment history and sense of time plays no role in the pace of decision-making regarding the child. (Tweet it!)

Poverty

75% of young adults reported good health, although studied aged out foster kids report more limiting health conditions than the national sample. (Tweet it!)

33% of studied aged out foster kids had no health insurance, double the national rate. (Tweet it!)

33% of studied aged out foster kids had incomes at or below the poverty level, a figure three times that of the national poverty rate. (Tweet it!)

Poverty, hopelessness and apathy are the conditions that coexist with foster care. (Tweet it!)

Foster care harms those in our society who can least afford to be harmed, battered souls who can't fend off poverty, tragedy, and misery. (Tweet it!)

Foster care takes your childhood. (Tweet it!)

Are we doing them more harm than good placing children in foster care? (Tweet it!)

"We are normal kids in abnormal circumstances." (Tweet it!)

The system pulls children from harm's way and then deserts them (Tweet it!)

Foster care is, as one child put it "punishment for something you didn't do" (Tweet it!)

"No one listens to foster children" and if they did listen, it's doubtful they would hear them or believe them. (Tweet it!)

Over 25% of study participants in aged out kids were categorized as "food-insecure". (Tweet it!)

Sibling separation

"If you call your siblings in traditional families, you can talk to them, in the foster care system, you have to argue why it's necessary." (Tweet it!)

Siblings in care. The foster system seems unable or unwilling to keep track of families and did not appear to have the resources to find them. (Tweet it!)

"I wasn't able to talk to my little brother for like 5 or 6 years." **Foster kid about brother in a different foster home.** (Tweet it!)

Many foster children have been separated not only from their parents, but from their siblings. (Tweet it!)

Secrecy

Every state cloaks its foster care system in secrecy, prohibiting disclosure of information about children's experiences in foster care. (Tweet it!)

Secrecy statutes enacted to protect children, routinely are used by state officials to conceal illegal and unconscionable practices. (Tweet it!)

The foster care system is cloaked in secrecy. Where there is institutional secrecy there are institutional abuses (Tweet it!)

Foster care abuse largely unchecked because the victims seldom complain the people who run the system hide behind confidentiality laws. (Tweet it!)

Confidentiality laws are based in the best and noblest of intentions but largely serve to protect officials (Tweet it!)

Foster care is made up of fifty secretive and byzantine state systems. (Tweet it!)

Secrecy laws (confidentiality laws) prohibit the official disclosure of any information about children's experiences in foster care. (Tweet it!)

Foster care is kept out of sight of the average American. The foster care system is protected by a benign image as helping society (Tweet it!)

Dissent in foster care is dealt with quickly and harshly. (Tweet it!)

Sexual Abuse

In Maryland in the 1990s, sexual abuse of foster children was four times higher than that found among the general population. (Tweet it!)

Arizona, a class action suit alleged that over 12% of the states foster care population were sexually abused while in care. (Tweet it!)

Model foster care programs in the Pacific Northwest, 24% of foster girls in survey said they were victims of sexual abuse(Tweet it!)

Teen birth

60% of former foster females will give birth while still a teen. (Tweet it!)

One of the ironies is that a significant percentage of foster care children themselves come from homes headed by single parents. (Tweet it!)

Withdrawal

The fostered child doesn't see themselves reflected in the family, and never stops trying to figure out how to be in the family. (Tweet it!)

Most people live under the dictum "Carpe diem" for foster children its "Carpe diem.... quam minimum credula postero." Seize the day, but put no trust in tomorrow (Tweet it!)

Foster Child: "I don't want to get attached to anything. Things maybe, because I know that's fine. But like people? No." (Tweet it!)

Here's the bottom line on foster care: society can pay some now or billions later in crime, drugs, addiction, jails, and welfare dependence (Tweet it!)

UNEMPLOYMENT

A federal study of former foster care wards; 40% were on public assistance and half were unemployed. (Tweet it!)

Estimate 49% of people who grew up in foster care will be chronically unemployed. (Tweet it!)

25% People who grew up in foster care will be homeless for at least one night (Tweet it!)

Only 17% of people who grew up in foster care are ever completely self-supporting. (Tweet it!)

Employment of studied aged out foster kids was found to be "sporadic", with 90% earning less than $10,000 over the past year. (Tweet it!)

Aged out adults were twice as likely as those remaining in care to be unemployed and out of school and three times more likely than the national sample. (Tweet it!)

The employment rate for studied aged out kids was 80%, compared to 95% for same-aged members of the general population. (Tweet it!)

Less than half of all former foster children are employed in any capacity four years after they age out of the system. (Tweet it!)

HOW TO FIX THE SYSTEM

Always remember: *The foster care system itself is based in the best and noblest of intentions*
(Tweet it!)

Annual Assessment

Doctor

Therapist

A pediatrician & psychologist should be included in the child's comprehensive assessment which should be done, by law, annually (Tweet it!)

Therapy & Healing

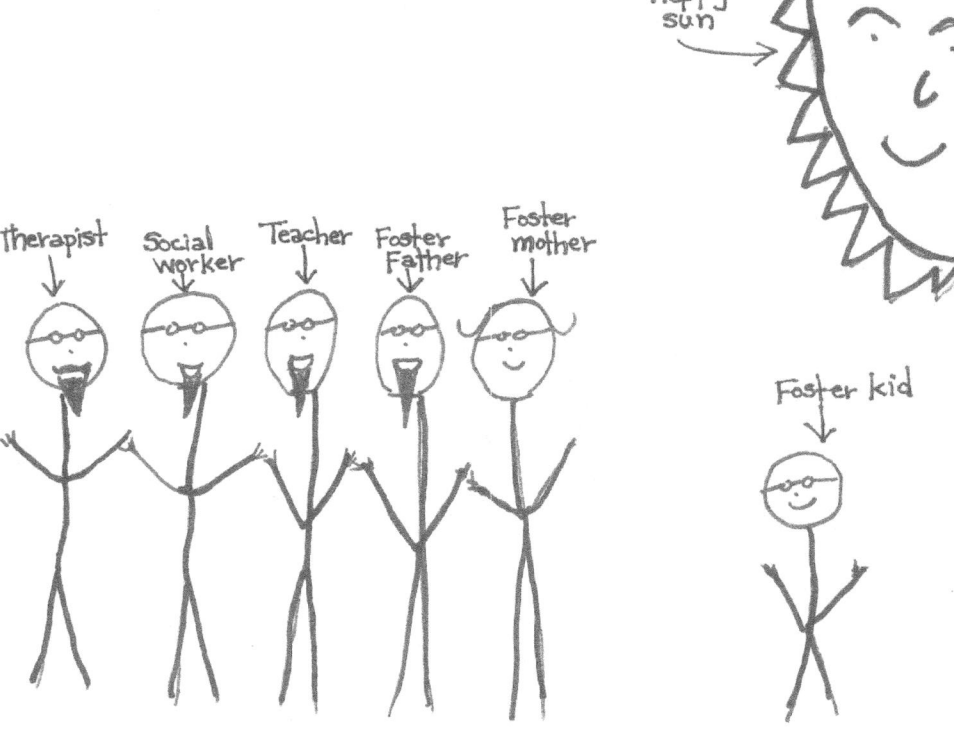

Temporary foster care should be a therapeutic time for foster kids not purgatory. (Tweet it!)

Foster care placement needs to be redirected to a healing experience for the child and not simply a place that offers room and board. (Tweet it!)

Improve permanency

More needs to be done to improve the system so that all children in foster care achieve permanency with families. (Tweet it!)

More needs to be done to ensure that proper support is in place for those who may age out of the system without a permanent family. (Tweet it!)

Include former foster children in under the protection of the Individuals with Disabilities Act. (Tweet it!)

Burned out case workers

Case workers burn out and leave the profession in very high numbers. (Tweet it!)

The annual turnover rate in the child welfare workforce is more than 20%. (Tweet it!)

The recommended number of cases for a social worker is 17. In some states, the number is three or four times that number. (Tweet it!)

Lighten social workers' caseloads to the recommended number of under 20. (Tweet it!)

Pay caseworkers a fair and reasonable salary. What they get now is a joke. (Tweet it!)

Redirected Financing

Federal funds for children in foster care has been unlimited, those funds could be used to provide in-home services to keep families together. (Tweet it!)

The Fed. Govt. should reward states for reducing the number of children in foster care and achieving permanence. (Tweet it!)

Make all children eligible for federal foster care support. You have the power to make that happen (Tweet it!)

If the US used less than 1% of foreign aid to pay foster parents better, a 3rd of the problems associated with foster care would end. (Tweet it!)

Fed. IV-E financing incentives favor foster care over other services that could keep families together (Tweet it!)

Addressing the inflexibility of federal IV-E is critical to ensure caseworkers deliver services tailored to the needs of the child (Tweet it!)

In most states, relatives and others who become legal guardians for foster kids lose fin. assistance when the child exits foster care (Tweet it!)

Estimated 20,000 children in long-term arrangements with relatives could leave foster care if federal funds could support guardianship. (Tweet it!)

A federal financing system with increased flexibility and accountability is a way to prevent children from languishing in foster care. (Tweet it!)

Change the way the federal government's child welfare finances services children in foster care and that will change everything. (Tweet it!)

Establish a federal foster care financing system that states can rely on to be sufficient and flexible. (Tweet it!)

Help more children leave foster care by supporting federal guardianships for relatives and other caregivers.

Stop restricting federal funds to supporting children in out-of-home foster care placements, it should not pay to keep families apart. (Tweet it!)

Give incentives to prevent the need for foster care, reconnect youth with family, or find new families through adoption or guardianship. (Tweet it!)

Compensate foster parents more fairly and in return demand they keep children, even when they act out. (Tweet it!)

Keep children in touch with sibling

"Having family helps with identity formation, a sense of belonging, and the security of knowing that no matter what, you will always have a place to go**." Sarah Greenblatt** (Tweet it!)

"Having family to care about them can be the single most healing experience for many youth in foster care." **Sarah Greenblatt, Casey Family Services** (Tweet it!)

Helping children transition out of foster care

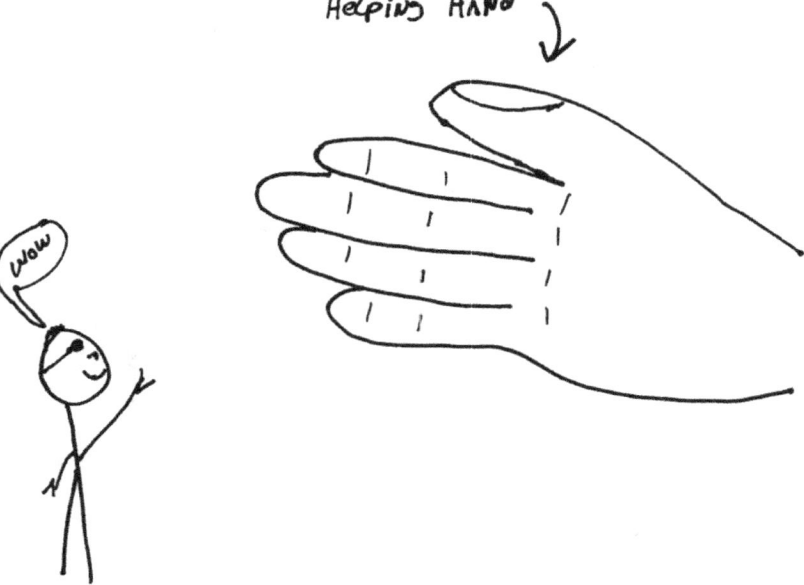

It would be fair to include former foster children under the protection of the Individuals with Disabilities Act. (Tweet it!)

Extend foster care and Medicaid eligibility up to age 21 for all youth in care. (Tweet it!)

Provide services under the Chafee Foster Care Independence Act to all youth who leave care, not just youth aging out. (Tweet it!)

Reform the federal foster care financing system to improve permanency outcomes for children to save kids aging out. (Tweet it!)

As bad as it is, Kinship care is better than foster care

Nearly a quarter of all children currently in foster care live with relatives. (Tweet it!)

Children placed with licensed relatives increased in the 1980s, from 18% to 30% in 1990. For the past 10 years, the number is at 24%. (Tweet it!)

It's estimated that approximately 150,000 foster care children are living with relatives. (Tweet it!)

When relatives provide foster care (known as kinship care), siblings can often stay together. (Tweet it!)

Kinship care improves stability by keeping displaced children closer to their extended families, their neighborhoods, and their schools. (Tweet it!)

Informal kinship care is far more common than formal kinship care. (Tweet it!)

The rate foster kids placed with licensed relative varies some states placing less than 10% others placing more than 40% (Tweet it!)

Most kinship parents are grandmothers or other close relatives. (Tweet it!)

Kinship caregivers are predominately families of color. (Tweet it!)

Black children are four to five times more likely than white non-Hispanic children to live in kinship care settings. (Tweet it!)

Kinship foster care families tend to have limited incomes. (Tweet it!)

Kinship caregivers tend be unmarried, less-educated, unemployed, live in poverty, receive government social welfare programs. (Tweet it!)

Kinship foster care families have less formal contact with social workers than traditional foster families. (Tweet it!)

Kinship foster care families are much less likely to adopt the children in their care than non-relative foster families. (Tweet it!)

Only 8% of in kinship foster care are adopted. (Tweet it!)

Research suggests that kinship care offers greater stability for children who are living with their relatives (Tweet it!)

Older children (ages six to 17) are more likely to live in kinship care settings than are younger children (under five). (Tweet it!)

In 2004, there was a total of 153,000 licensed/certified/approved kinship and non-relative foster homes nationwide. (Tweet it!)

In 2005, 24% of youth living in foster care were residing with their relatives. (Tweet it!)

PARENTAL RIGHTS AND RULES FOR REUNITED PARENT

The connection between the biological parents and child is ancient, mystical, primal, and mysterious. It outlasts all things. (Tweet it)

Special caution must be taken to ensure that fostering families and/or the social worker doesn't work against reunification (Tweet it)

Open court proceedings involve the removal of children from their parents, and child guardianship cases. (Tweet it!)

Older youth who maintain close ties with his or her birth parents may not want those parental rights terminated. (Tweet it!)

It's not appropriate to terminate parental rights of a parent with disabilities who physically cannot parent but wants to...it happens. (Tweet it!)

A parent should be required, by federal law, to perform a set of tasks before they can be reunified with their children. (Tweet it!)

Only reunite a parent after a course on abuse, mental health & parenting, demo proficiency in parenting & anger management. (Tweet it!)

Reunited parents should also be required to maintain adequate housing, demonstrate financial ability to provide for their child. (Tweet it!)

If a reunited parent fails to meet any relatively easy requirements for reunitement the state should terminate their parental rights (Tweet it!)

If a reunited parent fails to meet any easy requirements for reunitement require them to pay a portion of the cost of the childs care (Tweet it!)

The first role of the social workers should be focused on helping children find safe, permanent families. (Tweet it!)

Children in relative foster care homes reunify at a slower rate than children in other placements. (Tweet it!)

44 % (or about 241,000 children) have reunification with their birth families as their case goal. (Tweet it!)

On average, children stay in the system for almost three years (31 months) before either being reunited with their families or adopted. (Tweet it!)

Almost 20 % wait five years or more before either being reunited with their families or adopted. (Tweet it!)

54% of the young people leaving the system in 2005 were reunified with their birth parents or primary caregivers. (Tweet it!)

Among states, the rate of children being reunified with their families in 1 yr. of entering foster care is from a high of 76% to low 30% (Tweet it!)

The median length of stay in foster care for children before they are reunified is six months. (Tweet it!)

Infants are less likely to be reunified with their birth families than older children, but more likely to be adopted. (Tweet it!)

Children removed because they were neglected are reunified with their families at a lower rate than other children. (Tweet it!)

Black and/or Hispanic children are less likely to be reunified with their families than other children in the foster care system. (Tweet it!)

The longer a child is in out-of-home care, the less likely reunification will be achieved. (Tweet it!)

Over 60% of infants under age 1 had a case goal of reunification, compared to less than half of children six years and older. (Tweet it!)

Kids reunified within a year of being in foster care without proper support for birth parents, are more likely to reenter foster care. (Tweet it!)

Children under a year old are reunified with their parents only 35% of the time. (Tweet it!)

68% of Asian children are reunified, as are 54% of whites, 58% Hispanics, 54% American Indians; for black children the rate is 48 %. (Tweet it!)

one-third of children who reunify with their parents re-enter foster care within three years. (Tweet it!)

Recognize the rights of foster children in writing

Foster children have the right to be protected from abuse, neglect, or other maltreatment in foster care (Tweet it!)

Foster parents and facility staff must be properly monitored and screened. (Tweet it!)

Any alleged maltreatment must be quickly and thoroughly investigated. (Tweet it!)

Foster children have the right to adequate food, clothing, and shelter. (Tweet it)

Foster children have the right to an appropriate, stable placement in the least restrictive situation possible. (Tweet it!)

Foster children have the right to regular medical and dental care, and any necessary mental health services. (Tweet it!)

Foster children have the right to needed developmental and educational services. (Tweet it)

Foster children have the right to case-planning services and a permanent home consistent with the purposes of their custody. (Tweet it!)

Foster children have the right not to deteriorate while in state custody. (Tweet it!)

Foster children have the right not to be discriminated against based on race, religion, or gender. (Tweet it!)

Other stuff we (that includes you) must do to end this nightmare

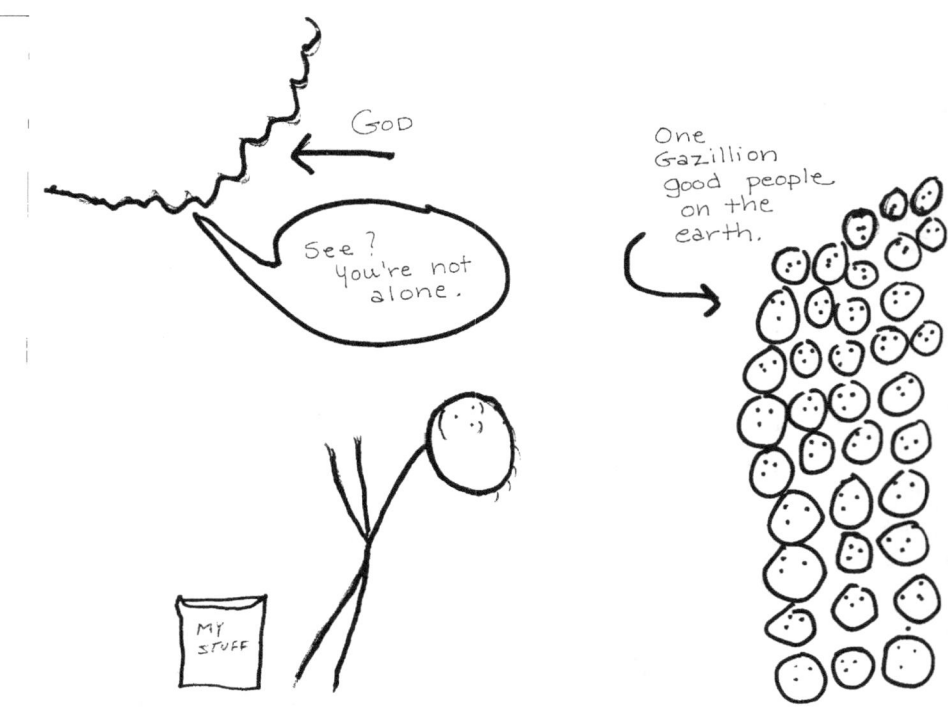

Make foster care a national priority. (Tweet it!)

There is no national approach or policy regarding child welfare in this country. (Tweet it!)

The system should keep children's time in foster care to a minimum and find new permanent families quickly for kids who can't return home. (Tweet it!)

The systems must provide adequate services — including education, medical services, and mental health care. (Tweet it!)

The systems must maintain a pool of available foster/adoptive homes so kids aren't housed in group homes, institutions, emergency shelters (Tweet it!)

The systems must provide better training for caseworkers to make appropriate decisions about the safety of children in foster homes. (Tweet it!)

The systems must streamline their management for maximum efficiency/ accountability. (Tweet it!)

The systems must improve/implement systems for data collection/analysis to pinpoint internal problems (Tweet it!)

Experts agree that the best thing to do is to leave the children at home if possible and provide good services to help the family cope. (Tweet it!)

Provide a group of professionals (therapist, pediatrician, social worker, tutor) to provide "wraparound services"(Tweet it!)

Offer services to children aging out of the system (Tweet it!)

Place foster children near their parents, or with extended family whenever possible (Tweet it!)

THE BOTTOM LINE............. We cannot build a future for foster children, but we can build foster children for the future. (Tweet it!)

THE LAST WORD............." I hope all of you were hearing what we had to say, because you are in a position to make things different." **Foster kid to the California Senate** (Tweet it!)

The tragedy of foster care is run by my government with my taxes but without my consent. NOT IN MY NAME. Reform Foster Care NOW (Tweet it!)

"But we can perhaps remember, if only for a time, that those who live with us are our brothers, that they share with us the same short moment of life; that they seek, as do we, nothing but the chance to live out their lives in purpose and in happiness, winning what satisfaction and fulfillment they can. Surely, this bond of common faith, this bond of common goal, can begin to teach us something." **Robert F. Kennedy**

Visit Our Home Page At:

http://www.fosterkidsstory.com/ (Tweet it!)

Visit our blog spots.

Foster kids own story
http://fosterkidsownstory.blogspot.com/

Foster care legislation
http://fostercarelegislation.blogspot.com/

Murder, Death and Abuse in Foster Care
http://murderdeathandabuseinfostercare.blogspot.com/

Foster Childrens Blog
http://fosterchildrensblog.blogspot.com/

Angels and Saints in the Foster Care System
http://angelsandsaintsinthefostercare.blogspot.com/

Worldwide Foster Care
http://worldwidefostercare.blogspot.com/

Aging Out of the system
http://agingoutofthesystem.blogspot.com/

The Foster Children's Bill of Rights
http://thefosterchildrensbillofrights.blogspot.com/

Mount Saint John School
http://mountsaintjohnsschoolalumni.blogspot.com/